MUDDY

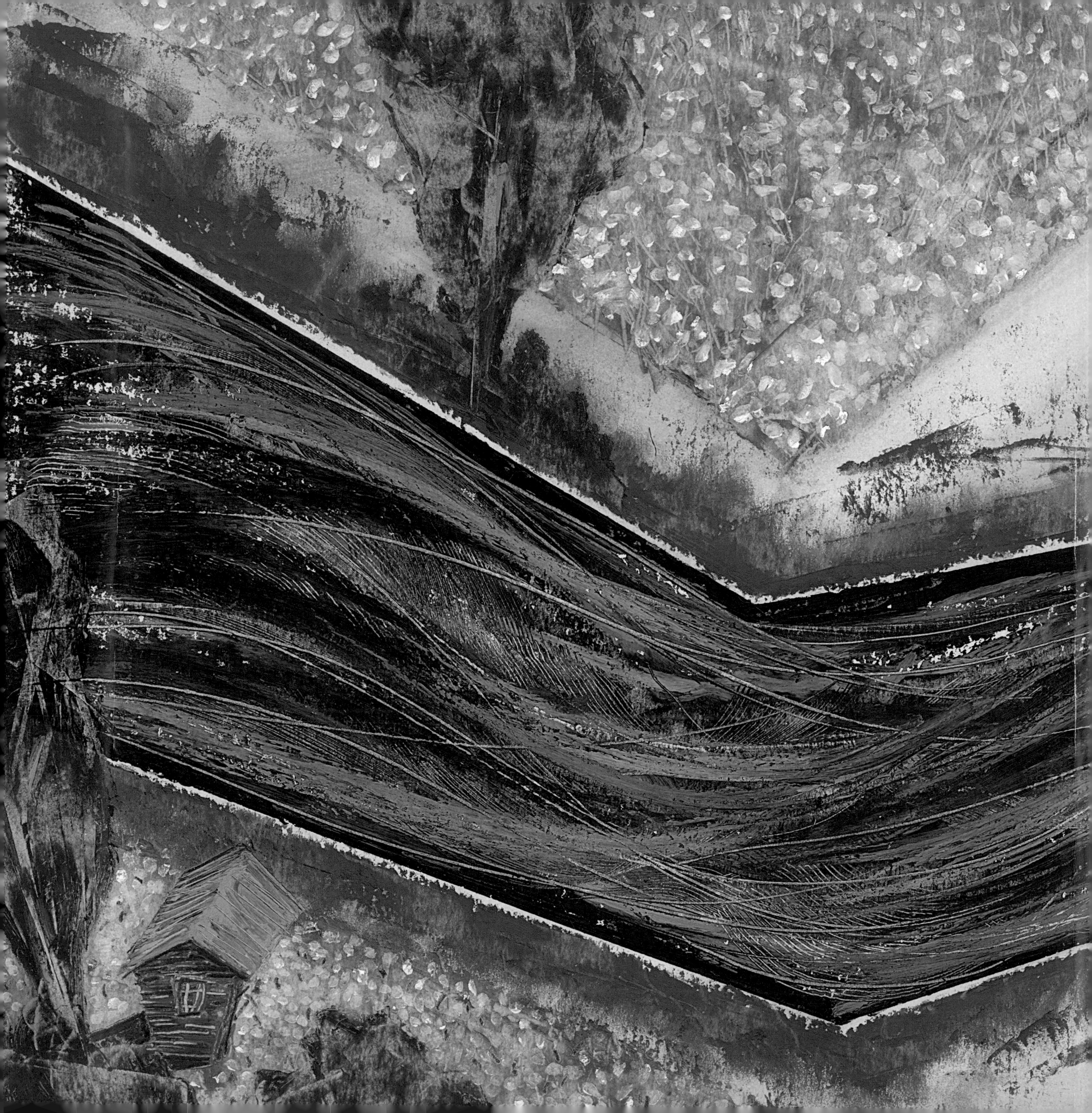

MUDDY

The Story of Blues Legend Muddy Waters

MICHAEL MAHIN

Illustrated by EVAN TURK

atheneum

Atheneum Books for Young Readers

New York London Toronto Sydney New Delhi

All "lyrics" and dialogue in the story represent the work of the author.

atheneum

ATHENEUM BOOKS FOR YOUNG READERS
An imprint of Simon & Schuster Children's Publishing Division
1230 Avenue of the Americas, New York, New York 10020

Photo on p. 47 by Paul Natikin/WireImage/Getty Images

Book design by Ann Bobco and Vikki Sheatsley. The text for this book was set in Gill Sans.
The illustrations for this book were rendered in watercolor, oil pastel,
china marker, printing ink, and newspaper collage.
Manufactured in China 0617 SCP
First Edition 10 9 8 7 6 5 4 3 2 1
Library of Congress Cataloging-in-Publication Data
Names: Mahin, Michael James, author. | Turk, Evan, illustrator.
Title: Muddy / Michael James Mahin ; illustrated by Evan Turk.
Description: New York ; London : Atheneum Books for Young Readers, 2016.
Includes bibliographical references and index. Identifiers: LCCN 2015045539 |
ISBN 978-1-4814-4349-4 (hc) ISBN 978-1-4814-4350-0 (eBook)
Subjects: LCSH: Muddy Waters, 1915–1983—Juvenile literature. |
Blues musicians—United States—Biography—Juvenile literature.
Classification: LCC ML3930.M92 M34 2016 | DDC 782.421643092—dc23
LC record available at http://lccn.loc.gov/2015045539

To my dad:
Sail on. Sail on.
—M. M.

To my parents
—E. T.

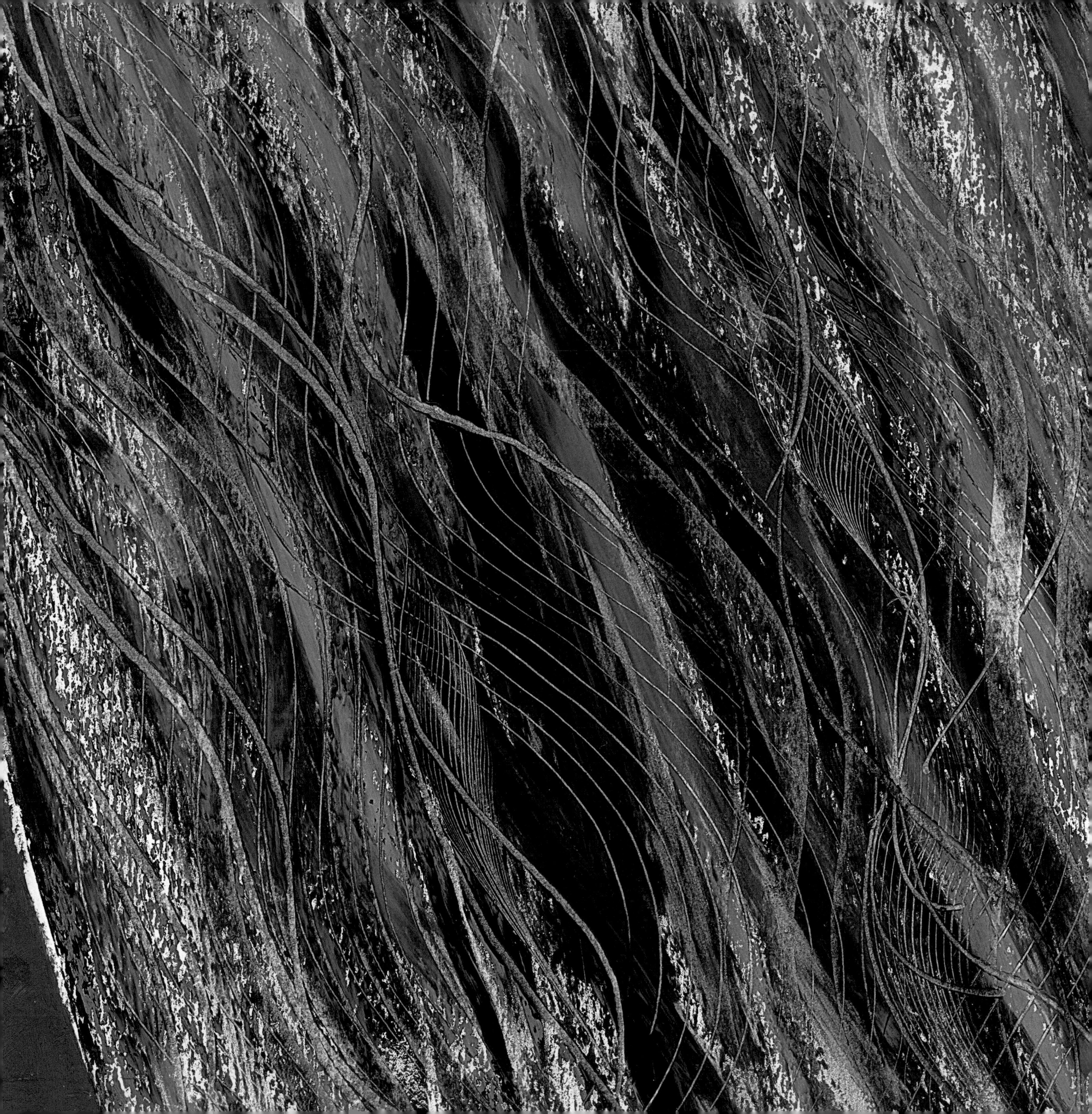

McKINLEY MORGANFIELD

was never good at doing what he was told.
Especially when it came to playing in the mud.
His mamma should've been mad. But she couldn't help but laugh.
"Ah, my muddy baby. My sweet, muddy baby."
McKinley's mamma gave him a life. And a laugh.
And then she was gone.
Forever.

Oh, child.
Long gone.
Oh, child.
Sail on.

But McKinley did have Grandma Della.
She scooped him up and tried to keep him clean
and finally just started calling him Muddy.

And he had music. Muddy loved the
"SAY IT WITH ME!" voice of the preacher,
and the "GLORY! GLORY!" singing of the choir.
But the music Muddy really loved,
they didn't play on Sundays.

What Muddy really loved was fish-fry music.
It was shake off the dust
and wring out your worries
and laugh and cry and feel alive music.
It was the blues, and Muddy couldn't get enough of it.

To have the blues was to feel bad.
But to play the blues was to take that low-down,
skunk-funk, deep-stomach hurt
and turn it into something else.

Muddy liked the blues.
Unfortunately,
Grandma Della did not.

Exchange!

"Last I checked, you can't eat the blues for breakfast," said Grandma Della. "No child of mine is gonna waste his time with music."

But Muddy was never good at doing what he was told.

So he found himself a half-smashed kerosene can to beat on.
And a wheezy accordion to squeeze.
And a tired piece of wire to pluck.
And made himself enough noise to feel good.
Not even Grandma Della could keep from dancing.

One night, Muddy watched his hero, blues legend Son House,
smash an empty bottle,
take the bottleneck,
and smooth its jagged edges over a fire.
"This is called a slide," he said, dragging the bottleneck up the strings.
The guitar howled like a wolf: powerful, lonely, and proud.
That was the sound of the Mississippi Delta.
That was the sound Muddy heard in his heart.

Muddy saved his pennies,
bought himself an old Stella guitar,
and practiced and played
for anyone who wanted to listen—
and a few who didn't.

After a long while, the howl
that was in his heart
finally started coming out
of his guitar.

On weekends, Muddy made the juke joints jump,
playing for the workers when it was time to unwind.

But when Monday came, Muddy was back in his overalls,
back working the fields.

Sharecropping was back-busting, soul-breaking work, and Muddy was already in a bad mood when the new boss man started picking on him. Muddy had gotten good at burying his anger and his pride and his hurt. To do otherwise could get you beaten up, or worse.

But today Muddy couldn't do it. He was tired of being picked on.
"I ain't a boy," he said. "And I sure ain't YOUR boy."

The boss man's face went red with anger as Muddy walked away.
"Stop right there or you'll never work in this town again!"
But Muddy was never good at doing what he was told.

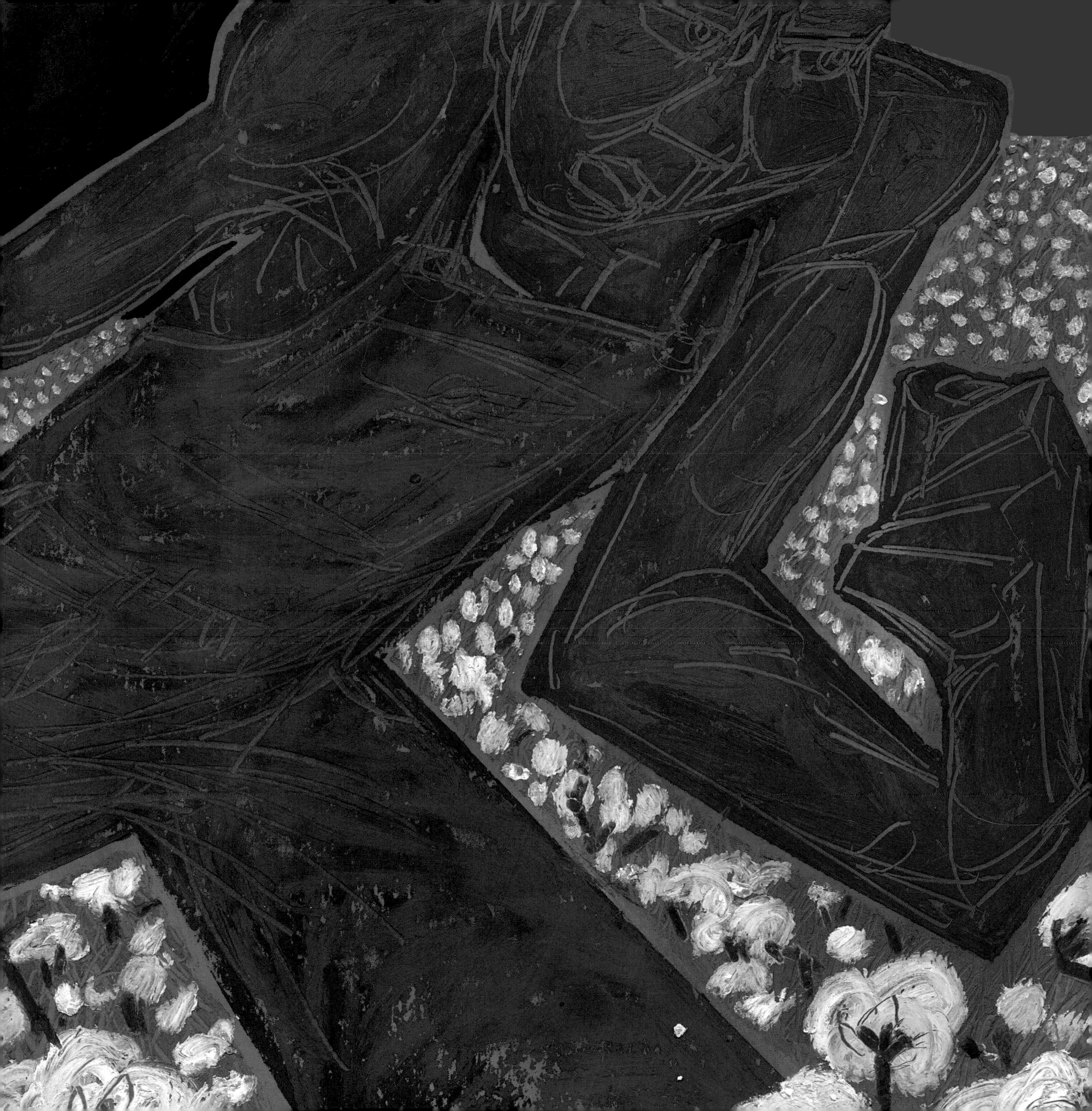

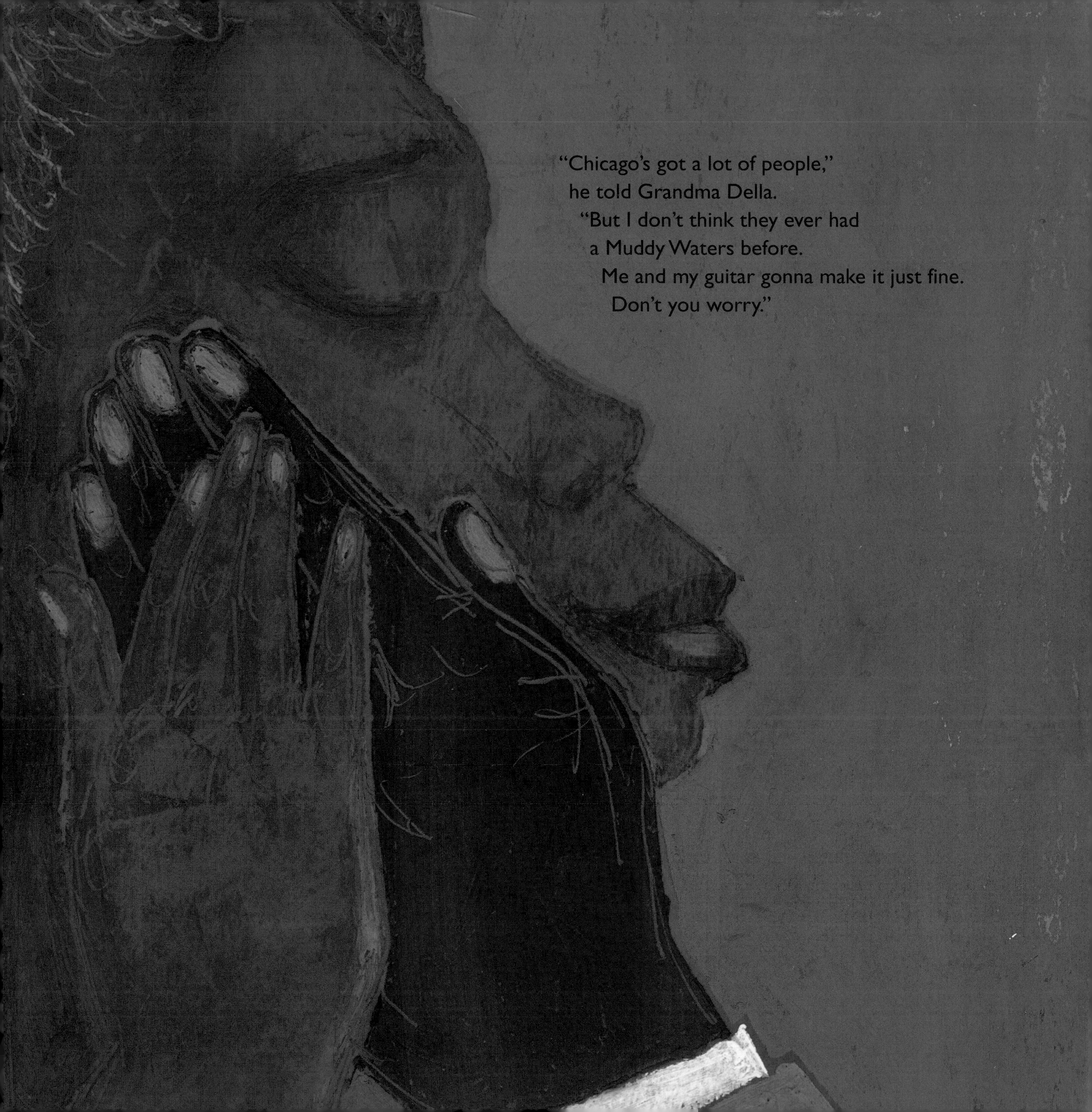

"Chicago's got a lot of people,"
he told Grandma Della.
"But I don't think they ever had
a Muddy Waters before.
Me and my guitar gonna make it just fine.
Don't you worry."

Clarksdale Coal &
And now the day has

Oh, child.
Long gone.
Oh, child.
Sail on.

The clack-a-track, steam-blur
of an Illinois Central train
rocketed Muddy and his guitar
into the bustle and buzz
of Chicago's South Side.

Chicago was plugged in,
turned on, and turned up.
And so was its music.
Records with electrified guitars
and jazzy horns were making the blues
jump all over town.

Chicago was the city of the
"Brown Bomber" Joe Louis,
the heavyweight boxing champion of the world.
It was the city of the *Chicago Defender*,
the legendary black newspaper
dedicated to fighting racial injustice.
And now it was the city of Muddy Waters.

In the clubs, the bebop jazzing swing of horns and strings
had laid itself down over the blues like a chiffon blanket.
This was music by city-smooth sophisti-cats, not country-dusted hound dogs.
No one wanted to hear a country boy playing country blues.
"You got to shake the dust off!" the club owners teased. "You got to jazz it up!"

But Muddy was never good
at doing what he was told.
The way he figured, his playing
was just fine. It was their hearing
that needed help. So Muddy
plugged in, turned on, turned up,
and out came the sound of the Delta,
buzzing and mad like an angry
hornet's nest looking for a fight.

It was a deep-feeling, gutbucket,
gut-aching music full of life
and love and trouble and pride.
It made people stand up
and raise their hands
and stomp their feet
and laugh and cry
and come alive.
It was nothing like the primped and
polished sounds people were used to.
And they loved it.

Whoa, yeah.
Whoa, yeah.
Sail on.
Sail on.

Muddy loved the clubs, but the late hours and low pay took their toll.
He couldn't live on change alone.

One day, Muddy got a call—a friend was making a record at the Universal Recording studios and he needed a sideman to back him up on guitar. If Muddy played well, they might even let him record his own song.

Finally, a chance.

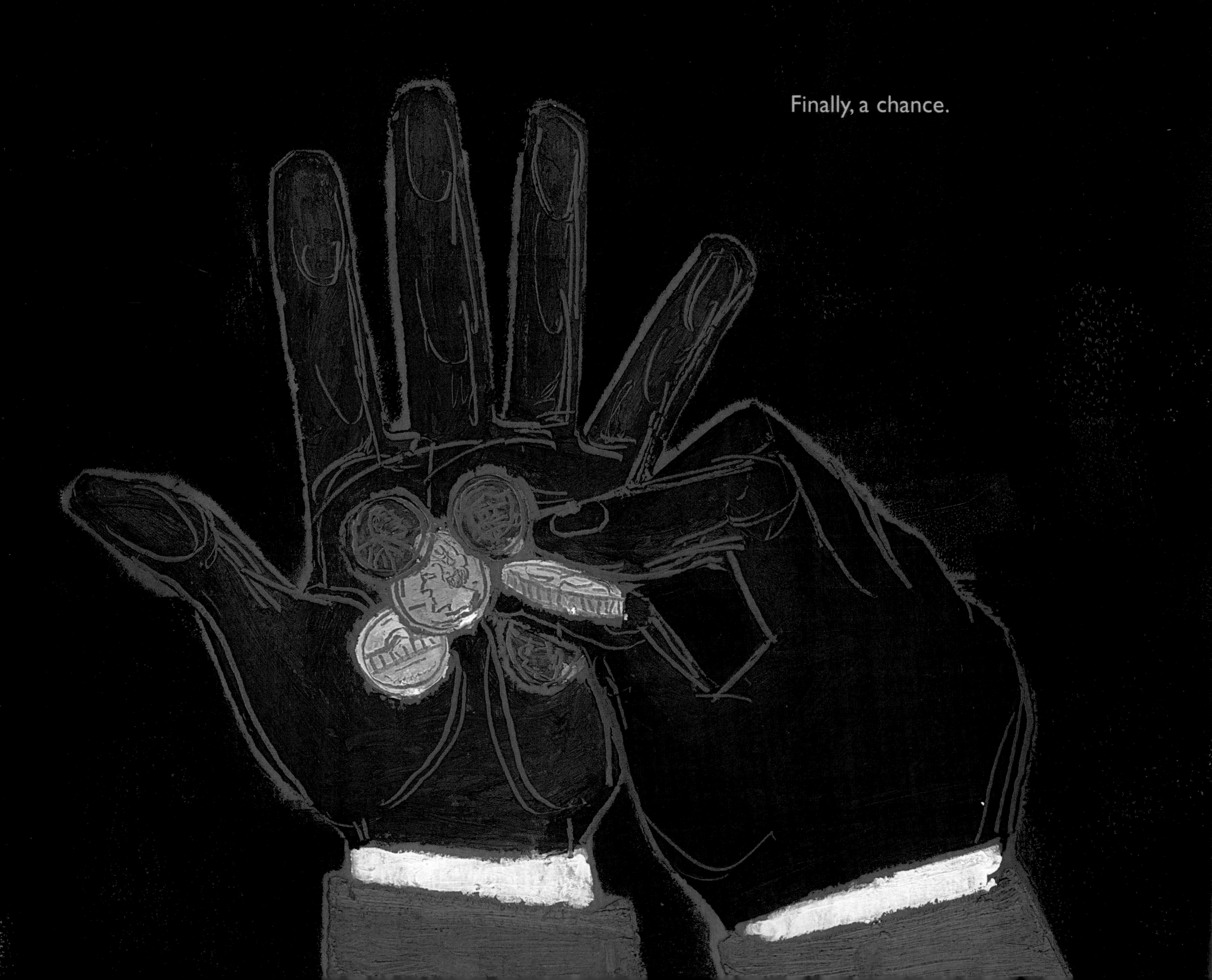

First they recorded his friend, and then they recorded him. Muddy did exactly what they told him to do. They added strings and horns and that soft and sweet Bluebird Records beat, but Muddy didn't care. He was just happy to be making a record.

James "Sweet Lucy
Carter
And his orchestra

Too bad they put someone else's name on it.
Muddy couldn't believe it. This was supposed to be his big break.
This was supposed to be *his* record. But it wasn't.
At least not according to the cover.

A year later, Muddy made a record for Columbia.
This time they got his name right. Too bad they decided
not to release the record.

Muddy was crushed. *I play it like they say to play it*
and they still don't like it, he thought.
What am I supposed to do?

When record producer Leonard Chess called, Muddy knew not to get his hopes up.
Leonard just wanted Muddy to record Leonard's music, Leonard's way.
But Muddy knew this might be his last chance, so he said yes.

"Soft is right, sweet and polite," said Leonard.
"That's where the cats are at."

Muddy picked up his guitar.
Walked to the microphone.
But he couldn't do it. Not again.

Muddy had never been
good at doing what
he was told, anyway.

When Leonard pointed
to the horns,
Muddy pointed to the exit.

"No horns. No jazz.
No fooling," said Muddy.
"If I'm going to fail,
I'm going to fail playing my music,
my way."

There was lightning in Muddy's eyes.
If Leonard could bottle that, maybe they'd
have something.

"You get one chance," said Leonard.
"Don't blow it."

Muddy sat down with his guitar. Pulled the microphone up close. And closed his eyes.

Whoa, child . . .

He remembered the dust, and the plow, and the meanness of the land,
and the softness of King Cotton.

Ohhh, child . . .

He called up the sticky heat of a summer night, the power of love, and the need for connection in a world that was so good at pulling people apart.

And he played just like Son House had taught him: not with his fingers, but with his heart. Muddy sang about life as he'd lived it, with all of its pain, its power, and its glory, forever.

Still unconvinced, Leonard printed only three thousand copies of the record and sent them to local stores.

Muddy chewed his nails and waited. What if people didn't like his voice? What if he wasn't good enough after all? Muddy didn't have to wait long to find out.

All across the South Side,
the boom and bounce of Muddy's voice
thundered down from open apartment windows.
People were talking. This new blues was something special.
It felt honest and raw. It felt real. It felt like the past and the future and the
country and the city all rolled into one.

Not only did Muddy have a record, he had a hit. In twenty-four hours, it was sold out.
Leonard printed more. A lot more.

Muddy Waters has shaped what has become
McKinley Morganfield's
Just Cryin' the Blues
Muddy Waters:
Muddy

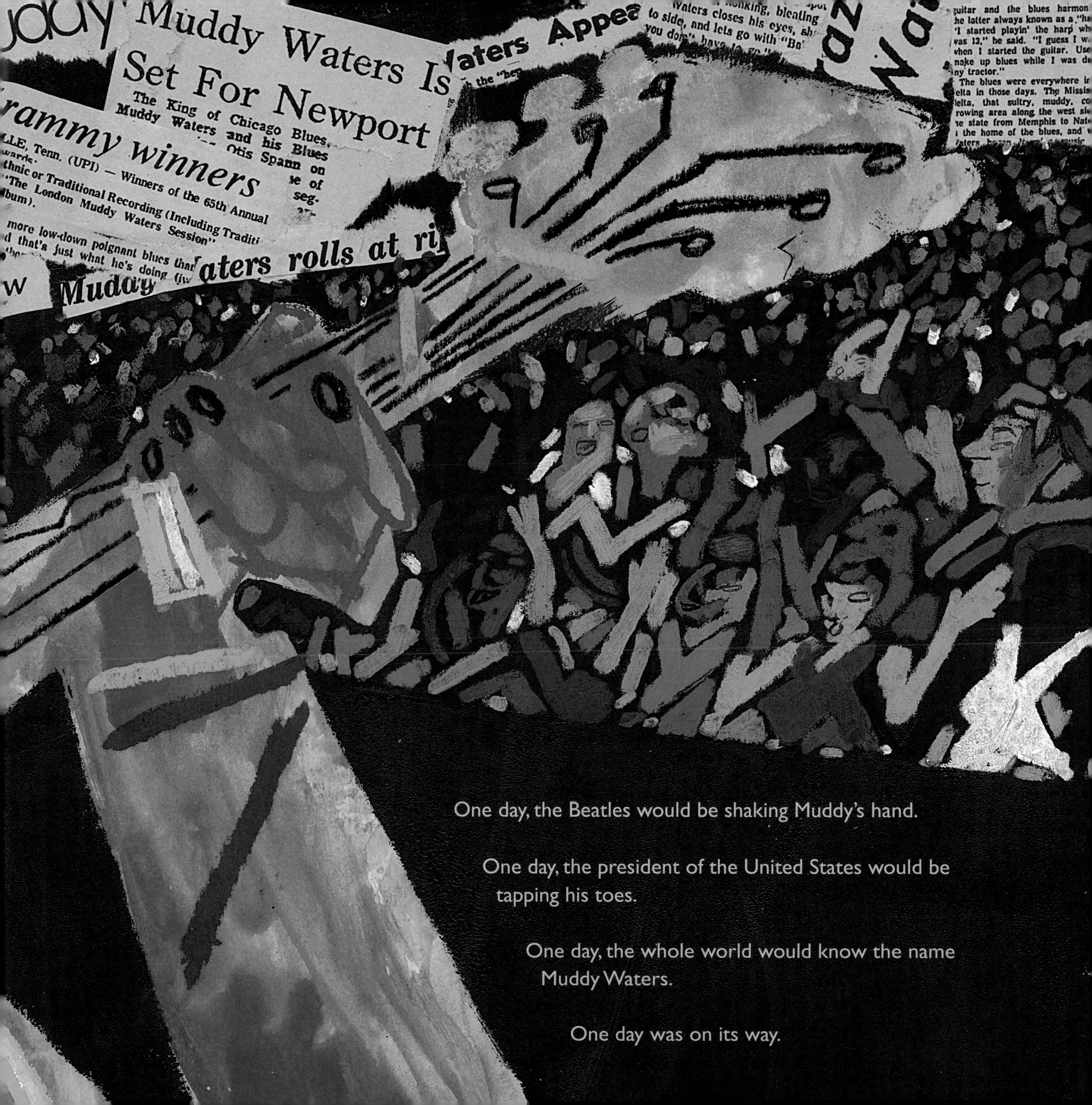

One day, the Beatles would be shaking Muddy's hand.

One day, the president of the United States would be tapping his toes.

One day, the whole world would know the name Muddy Waters.

One day was on its way.

Oh, child.
Long gone.
Oh, child.
Sail on.
We're sailing on.

Author's Note

When the Beatles came to the United States for the first time in 1964, they were about to become the biggest band in the world. They were asked whom they most wanted to meet. They could have said anyone. But they said, "Muddy Waters and Bo Diddley." The American reporters replied, "Muddy Waters? Where's that?" And the Beatles, witty as always, shot back, "Don't you know who your own famous people are here?"

Muddy Waters was born and raised along the western edge of Mississippi, in an area that included Issaquena, Rolling Fork, and Coahoma counties. In addition to being one of the poorest regions in the United States, this area was also heavily segregated, like most places in the South. Unfortunately for Muddy, racism was a part of everyday life.

While Muddy wasn't known to talk about the racism he experienced, one can assume that he, like millions of other African American men, women, and children, suffered greatly. It was this suffering, coupled with the hope for a better life, that led Muddy and six million other African Americans to leave the South in what is now known as the Great Migration.

Many, like Muddy, moved north to such cities as Chicago, Kansas City, and St. Louis in order to find work and escape the brutal racism of the southern states. This migration of African Americans to industrial centers gave rise to a new, black, urban culture that would exert enormous political, social, and artistic influence across the country in the years to come.

The musical genre known as "Chicago blues" is the style that Muddy helped invent, along with his early bandmates Jimmy Rogers, Little Walter, and Otis Spann. Muddy's genius was combining the rawness and emotion of the Delta blues with the urban sound and feel of the electric guitar and bass. While Muddy was not the only musician to do this, he quickly became one of the most influential. The instrumental composition of Muddy's bands—which always included a guitar, harmonica, piano, bass, and drums—laid the rhythmic and tonal foundation for what would become rock and roll.

In 1971, Muddy won his first of six Grammy Awards. Seven years later, he played for President Jimmy Carter at the White House. He is a member of the Rock & Roll Hall of Fame, as well as a recipient of the Grammy Lifetime Achievement Award.

Chuck Berry, Bob Dylan, Stevie Ray Vaughan, the Rolling Stones, Eric Clapton, Led Zeppelin, and countless others cite Muddy as a seminal influence. He is considered one of the most important artists in American music history, and is listed as number 17 on *Rolling Stone* magazine's 100 Greatest Artists list.

From the muddy shores of the Mississippi Delta to the polished parlors of Chicago, Muddy Waters's journey is a quintessentially American story of struggle, hope, determination, and perseverance. This book is an attempt to capture that spirit, and while some narrative elements are fictional, the author has been true to historical facts as much as possible.

Despite all of his achievements, Muddy did have one major regret in life: he never had a chance to go to school, and he never learned to read or write.

Bibliography

Gordon, Robert. *Can't Be Satisfied: The Life and Times of Muddy Waters.* New York: Little, Brown, 2002.

Rooney, James. *Bossmen: Bill Monroe & Muddy Waters.* New York: Da Capo Press, 1971.

Tooze, Sandra B. *Muddy Waters: The Mojo Man.* Ontario: ECW Press, 1997.

Further Listening

There are many great "Best of Muddy Waters" compilations. Here are a few:

The Best of Muddy Waters—The Millennium Collection (Chess, 1999)

Muddy Waters—The Definitive Collection (Geffen, 2006)

The Very Best of Muddy Waters (Epic/Legacy, 2011)

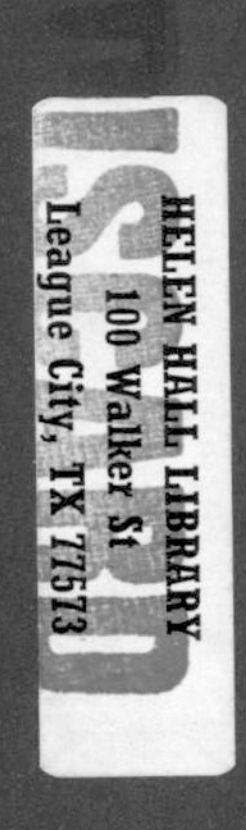